"THE ART OF NEGOTIATION:

Mastering the Deal for Career

and Financial Success"

Copyright Contents

TABLE OF CONTENT

Chapter 1: The Foundations of Negotiation

Negotiation is a more important element of our lives than we may think. Negotiation is the force that drives human relationships, decisions, and the global economy. It can be as simple as deciding where to go for dinner with a friend or as complex as closing a multimillion-dollar business deal.

In this chapter, we will go on a trip to investigate the foundations of negotiation—the foundations on which we will develop our capacity to master this art. Understanding the basic concepts of negotiation is critical whether you are an aspiring entrepreneur, a seasoned business executive, a parent dealing with an obstinate teenager, or anybody in between.

Why Does Negotiation Matter?

Negotiation is the art of achieving agreements, resolving conflicts, and navigating the complexities of human contact. It is the link that links many points of view, interests, and ambitions. But why is it so crucial, particularly in terms of professional and financial success?

Negotiation skills are frequently the deciding factor between those who receive a standard salary increase and those who secure a significant raise, a better job title, or more favorable working conditions. Your negotiation skills influence your professional development, the projects you work on, and your general job happiness.

Financial Success: Negotiation is essential in personal financial problems outside of the office. It may assist you in obtaining better bargains while purchasing a home, or a vehicle, or simply haggling for a reasonable price at a local market. Negotiation skills may also make a significant impact on investments and business initiatives, influencing your financial well-being.

Everyday Life: Negotiation goes beyond the professional and financial spheres. It's woven into the fabric of our daily interactions, from resolving family conflicts to reaching compromises with friends or coworkers. Learning to negotiate improves your effectiveness in these everyday situations, fostering better relationships and more fluid collaborations.

Understanding Negotiation Psychology

Negotiation is fundamentally a psychological game. It is the result of the interaction of perceptions, motivations, and emotions. To successfully navigate this complex terrain, it is critical to understand the psychological factors that influence the negotiation process.

Negotiation entails dealing with people, and people are inherently unique. Recognizing and appreciating these distinctions is critical. Everyone brings their own set of beliefs, biases, and emotional baggage to the table. Understanding human nature allows you to tailor your approach to the person with whom you are negotiating, making the process smoother and more productive.

Interests and Positions: Underlying interests often drive people's positions in negotiations. It is critical to distinguish between the two. Positions are the stated demands or offers, whereas interests are the underlying motivations for those positions. Effective negotiators look beyond the surface to identify the interests of both parties, seeking common ground and mutually beneficial solutions.

Communication: The way you communicate in a negotiation can significantly impact its outcome. Active listening, empathy, and effective expression are key components of successful communication. Being attuned to verbal and non-verbal cues allows you to gauge the emotional state of the other party and adjust your approach accordingly.

Cognitive Biases: Humans are susceptible to cognitive biases, which can cloud judgment and decision-making during negotiation. Familiarizing yourself with common biases, such as anchoring, confirmation bias, and overconfidence, can help you both recognize and mitigate these biases in yourself and your counterpart.

The Importance of Preparation

Successful negotiation is not merely a product of charisma and quick thinking. It's rooted in thorough preparation. Preparation is the key to understanding the context, setting clear objectives, and developing a robust strategy for your negotiations.

Setting Clear Objectives: Before entering a negotiation, you must define your goals and objectives. What do you aim to achieve? Whether it's a higher salary, a successful business deal, or resolving a personal dispute, having a clear sense of your objectives provides direction and focus during the negotiation.

Information Gathering: Information is power in negotiation. The more you know about the other party, their needs, constraints, and preferences, the better equipped you are to negotiate effectively. Research and gather relevant information to bolster your position and enhance your understanding of the negotiation's dynamics.

Developing a Negotiation plan: Every negotiation should be addressed with a well-thought-out plan. This strategy should consider the desired outcome, the interests of both parties and potential areas of compromise. It's a blueprint that guides your activities throughout the negotiation, helping you keep control and react to changing conditions.

BATNA (Best Alternative to a Negotiated Agreement): Understanding your BATNA is vital. Your BATNA is the course of action you will take if the negotiation doesn't lead to a satisfactory agreement. Knowing your BATNA offers a safety net, helping you to bargain from a position of power.

Negotiation as an Art Form

Negotiation isn't a mechanical procedure but rather an art form that needs creativity, adaptation, and finesse. It requires the strategic application of the concepts we've studied so far, together with a profound grasp of human behavior.

As we advance in our investigation of the art of bargaining, we'll dig into particular strategies and real-life settings, from the boardroom to the family room. Whether you're pursuing job progress or looking for financial success, these ideas will serve as the basis upon which you'll build your bargaining skills. Remember, negotiating is more than a talent; it's a way of life, a gateway to unlocking possibilities, and a method to control your future.

Chapter 2: The Power of Preparation

In the realm of negotiation, success is decided by more than just the words you use throughout the engagement. What occurs before the negotiation starts typically influences the result. The emphasis of this chapter is on preparation, which is the foundation of good negotiation.

The Importance of Having Specific Goals

Assume you're planning a cross-country road vacation. Would you go on a trip without a certain destination in mind? Negotiation follows the same logic. To be effective, you must have specific goals. These goals serve as your destination, directing your negotiating trip and guaranteeing a meaningful and beneficial end.

Defining Your Objectives:

The first stage in preparing is to identify your goals. You must have a clear knowledge of your objectives, whether in your professional position, personal life, or commercial affairs. For example, if you're negotiating a raise, your target may be a specified percentage increase or a minimum yearly income. When purchasing a home, your objective may be to secure the property at a certain price range.

Objective Prioritization:

You may have many goals in certain talks. It is critical to prioritize them. Which goals are unassailable, and which are amenable to compromise? Setting these goals allows you to make educated judgments throughout the negotiating process. You'll understand when to be forceful and when to seek common ground.

Understanding the Difference Between Interests and Positions:

It's critical to differentiate between interests and stances while setting goals. During a negotiation, positions are the explicit demands or offers presented. In contrast, interests are the fundamental impulses that drive such attitudes. While beliefs are often fixed, interests are more malleable.

Consider the following scenario: Assume you're bargaining with a vendor for a cheaper price on a large order of goods for your company. Your stance is that you would want a 10% discount. However, your overarching goal is to save money to increase your company's profitability. You may be more flexible in your bargaining technique if you grasp the difference between your position (the 10% discount) and your interest (improved profitability).

The Benefit of Information

Information is a sort of money in negotiations. The more you have, the more powerful you are in negotiations. Information may empower you by providing insights into the requirements, preferences, and restrictions of your counterpart. It also allows you to make more educated selections throughout the negotiating process.

Investigating the Other Party:

Spend time investigating the opposite side before going into a discussion. Understanding the history aims, and historical behavior in comparable discussions of a firm, a person, or a department within your organization may give significant information. For example, while negotiating with a possible business partner, knowing their history, financial soundness, and reputation might help you determine their dependability.

Understanding Needs and Limitations:

It's critical to understand the other party's demands and limits in addition to studying them. What are they attempting to accomplish in this negotiation, and what difficulties could they encounter? Knowing this information will allow you to modify your proposal to answer their worries, boosting the chances of a successful conclusion.

Data Analysis in the Market:

Market data may be a significant tool depending on the nature of your negotiation. Understanding market trends and industry norms may give a firm basis for your arguments whether purchasing a home, establishing a wage, or negotiating the pricing of products and services. It enables you to compare expectations and support your suggestions.

Internal Data Collection:

You'll also need internal information in many circumstances. Budget limits, corporate rules, or team dynamics are examples of this. Access to this information may assist you in making better-informed choices and avoiding making obligations that your company will be unable to meet.

Making a Negotiation Strategy

A negotiator should not begin a negotiation without a strategy, just as a general would not enter a battlefield without a well-planned war plan. Your strategy serves as a road map for your activities during the negotiating process. It considers your aims, the facts you've obtained, and negotiating psychology.

Strategy Based on Goals:

Your negotiating technique should be an exact representation of your goals. It describes how you intend to attain your objectives, taking into consideration possible obstacles and areas of flexibility. For example, if you want to get a new job with a better income, you may highlight your existing successes, investigate industry compensation norms, and emphasize the unique value you provide to the firm.

Risk Evaluation:

Identifying possible risks and difficulties is a vital component of your plan. What challenges may you face, and how can you overcome them? For instance, if you're negotiating better terms with a supplier, your risk assessment may include analyzing the probability of supply chain interruptions and preparing contingency measures.

Developing Relationships and Trust:

Building rapport and trust during a negotiation may be a smart strategy. This is especially vital if you have a long-term or continuous connection with the other person. Steps should be taken in your approach to develop a good working relationship. Building trust may result in more efficient and cooperative bargaining.

Preparing for counterarguments:

Successful negotiators anticipate counterarguments and prepare replies in advance. You may be prepared with compelling, well-thought-out replies if you analyze probable objections or alternative suggestions. This proactive strategy strengthens your position and you maintain your cool throughout the discussion.

Adaptability and adaptability:

A well-thought-out approach should also allow for flexibility and adaptability. Conditions may change as the discussions advance. Your plan should allow for alterations while remaining focused on your overall goals. Keep in mind that flexibility does not suggest weakness; rather, it displays your adaptability and response.

BATNA: Your Security Net

BATNA is an acronym that stands for "Best Alternative to a Negotiated Agreement." Your BATNA is your backup plan—the action you'll take if the negotiation does not result in a satisfying agreement. It acts as a safety net, providing you with confidence and a clear route if the negotiation does not go as planned.

Choosing Your BATNA:

Before beginning any negotiation, you must first define your BATNA. What will you do if you and the other side are unable to reach an agreement? This might be looking into other employment opportunities if a pay negotiation breaks through, or looking into different suppliers if you can't reach an agreement with your existing vendor.

Increasing Your Negotiating Power:

A strong BATNA increases your negotiation strength. If you have a good alternative, you may confidently press for better terms in the negotiation. If your BATNA is poor, you may need to **be more flexible throughout the negotiation to prevent an unhappy conclusion**

Preventing Desperation:

Knowing your BATNA helps you avoid making rash judgments. If you have a realistic alternative, you are less inclined to accept poor conditions or to capitulate too early. This information allows you to retain a strong negotiation stance.

In summary, the strength of preparation resides in establishing clear goals, acquiring facts, forming a strong negotiating strategy, and comprehending your BATNA. These procedures serve as the basis for effective negotiations. In the next chapters, we'll look at particular negotiating approaches, but keep in mind that your preparation is the foundation for these strategies. By devoting time and effort to preparation, you arm yourself with the tools and information needed to navigate the negotiating process with confidence and ability.

Chapter 3: Building Strong Relationships

Negotiation is often portrayed as a war of wits, a conflict of competing interests in which one side triumphs and the other loses. However, this is a limited picture of a complex process that extends beyond simple money transactions. Successful negotiations are about more than simply getting the best offer; they are also about developing and sustaining meaningful connections. This chapter digs into the essence of negotiation, highlighting the value of trust, empathy, and clear communication. We will look at how these elements are important in effective negotiations and how they may lead to long-term relationships.

Beyond the Transaction: Relationships' Role

While the exact parameters of an agreement are often the focus of negotiation, the core of negotiation extends far deeper. Negotiations are dynamic exchanges between persons or parties that are rooted in human psychology, emotions, and relationships.

Understanding the larger context is essential. A good negotiation is not a one-time event, but rather a continuous process. You may find yourself bargaining with the same parties again, in either comparable or dissimilar circumstances. In your working life, the relationships you build during negotiations may have a long-term influence on your career.

The Three Relationship-Building Foundations:

Three fundamental components underlie connection development in the arena of negotiations:

Trust is the bedrock upon which every good connection is based. Negotiations are more efficient, transparent, and less combative when parties trust each other. Open conversation and productive problem-solving are enabled by trust.

Empathy is the capacity to comprehend and share another person's emotions. It's an effective negotiating strategy because it lets you perceive the situation through the eyes of your rival. Empathy fosters comprehension and may lead to innovative solutions that please both sides.

Effective Communication: Effective communication is essential for successful negotiations. This entails not only clearly expressing your own opinions and wants, but also carefully listening to what your opponent has to say. Good communication ensures that no critical information or issues are overlooked.

Let's take a closer look at each of these pillars and how they contribute to good negotiating interactions.

The Importance of Trust

Trust is the foundation of every lasting relationship, and it is no different in the context of negotiation. Negotiations are more likely to result in win-win solutions when trust is established. Parties are more open to working together, sharing information, and making compromises.

The Components of Trust:

Credibility: It is critical to be seen as credible. If your opponent feels you will keep your promises, they are more inclined to trust you. Credibility is based on a track record of fulfilling commitments and being truthful in your transactions.

Credibility and reliability are inextricably linked. You guarantee that you will always keep your promises. Trust is strengthened when your opponent understands they can rely on you.

Transparency entails being open and honest in your communication. Sharing knowledge, even if it is not immediately beneficial, fosters trust. When dealing with delicate issues, transparency is extremely important.

Consistency in conduct and communication is essential for trust. It assists your rival in anticipating your actions and answers. When you are unpredictable or chaotic in your interactions, trust is eroded.

Negotiation Trust Building:

Begin with Honesty: The best policy is honesty. Begin talks by being upfront and honest. If you are aware of any possible obstacles or restrictions in your idea, make them known. This openness sets the tone for a fair and trustworthy discussion.

Keep Promises and Commitments: During negotiations, keep any promises or commitments you make. Failure to follow your promise may seriously undermine trust.

Avoid Deception: While deception, such as making false statements or distorting facts, might provide immediate benefits, it often results in long-term harm to your reputation and credibility.

Demonstrate Understanding: Demonstrating an understanding of your counterpart's demands and concerns might help you create trust. The other side is more inclined to respond if they feel heard and respected.

The Importance of Empathy

Empathy is a powerful negotiating tool. It enables you to put yourself in the shoes of your counterpart and comprehend their feelings, motives, and points of view. This comprehension may result in more effective problem-solving and mutually beneficial agreements.

Empathy's Advantages:

Enhanced Understanding: Empathy allows you to understand your counterpart's underlying wants and feelings. This greater comprehension may lead to more innovative solutions that suit both sides.

Reduced Tension: When your adversary believes you really grasp their viewpoint, the tension in the negotiation might be reduced. They are more inclined to work together and find common ground.

Conflict Resolution: Empathy is a great tool for conflict resolution. It enables you to deal with emotional difficulties and assist in reconciliation, resulting in better relationships.

Mutual Respect: Approaching the discussion with empathy shows respect for the other side. This regard creates a favorable environment and increases the probability of a successful result.

Empathy Training:

Active listening entails paying great attention to what your coworker is saying. Active listening is not just hearing words but also comprehending the emotions and intentions behind them.

Ask Open-Ended Questions: By asking open-ended questions, you may encourage your opponent to express themselves. This encourages them to contribute more and gives you insight into their point of view.

Validate feelings: Recognize the feelings that your counterpart is feeling. This affirmation may assist in reducing emotional stress and foster a more collaborative environment.

Consider putting yourself in their shoes: Consider the problem from the perspective of your counterpart. What are their motives, worries, and fears? Understanding their point of view may help you decide how to proceed.

The Importance of Clear Communication

Any successful negotiation relies on effective communication. It entails openly communicating your own opinions and wants while also attentively listening to your adversary. Communication is a two-way street that is essential for communicating your message and comprehending the other party's message.

Effective Communication Elements:

Clarity: When you communicate clearly, you guarantee that your opponent knows your objectives and suggestions. Avoid jargon and complicated terminology.

Active listening is not just hearing words but also comprehending the emotions and intentions underlying them. It is also necessary to pay attention to nonverbal clues.

Courteous Tone: Keep your conversation courteous and professional. Avoid sarcasm, rudeness, or anger, since they may derail a productive discussion.

Request explanation: If anything is unclear or confusing, don't be afraid to request explanation. It is preferable to seek insight rather than create assumptions.

Building Effective Negotiation Communication:

Prepare and Organize Your Thoughts: Before engaging in a negotiation, organize your ideas and recommendations. This preparation will enable you to speak more clearly and convincingly.

Patience is a virtue: Your counterpart may need time to analyze information or make judgments. Allow them the space they need to speak properly.

Address Misunderstandings As Soon As Possible: If you notice a misunderstanding or miscommunication, address it as soon as possible. Clarify any areas of misunderstanding to ensure that the discussion runs well.

Chapter 4: The Art of Persuasion

Persuasion is your most potent friend in the delicate dance of negotiation. To master the art of negotiation, you must first become a powerful communicator, capable of persuading people and successfully articulating your views. Chapter 4 is your introduction to persuasive psychology—a deep dive into the factors that regulate human decision-making. In this section, we will look at numerous persuasive approaches, ethical issues, and strategies to help you become a more successful negotiator.

The Influence of Persuasion

The power to convince is at the foundation of good negotiation. It is the skill of persuading people to see things your way, accept your offers, and make decisions that accord with your aims. Persuasion in the context of negotiation is not about manipulation or deception; it is about presenting your argument most compellingly and persuasively possible.

Why Persuasion Is Important:

Influence and Decision-Making: Individuals make choices in negotiations, each with their own set of views, values, and interests. Persuasion is a strategy for bridging the gap between competing points of view and leading to mutually beneficial agreements.

Win-Win Situations: Effective persuasion may result in win-win situations in which both sides leave the bargaining table happy. It's not about one side winning and the other losing; it's about finding solutions that satisfy both sides' needs.

Improved Relationships: When utilized responsibly and professionally, persuasion may improve the connection between negotiating parties. The confidence and goodwill gained via effective bargaining may continue beyond the present transaction, opening the door to future cooperation.

Understanding Persuasion Psychology:

Human psychology serves as the basis for persuasion. It stems from our cognitive and emotional reactions to facts, arguments, and appeals. Understanding these psychological concepts allows you to successfully adjust your persuasive attempts.

Considerations for Ethical Behavior

Before delving into particular persuasive strategies, it's critical to address persuasion's ethical implications. Persuasion is a powerful weapon, but it must always be used with integrity and honesty. Ethical persuasion respects others' autonomy and dignity. Here are some general guidelines:

Transparency: Be open and honest in your communications. Present facts truthfully and without deception or manipulation.

Respect others' choices and decisions, especially if they vary from your own. Coercion or pressure has no place in ethical persuasion.

Empathy: Consider your counterpart's wants and emotions. Empathy enables you to construct convincing arguments that connect with their point of view.

Intent to Win: Seek solutions that benefit all parties involved. Finding mutually beneficial results is the goal of ethical persuasion.

Long-Term Relationships: Consider your options beyond the present discussion. Persuasion should help to develop solid, long-lasting connections.

Techniques of Persuasion

There are several persuasive strategies at your disposal in the field of negotiation. These strategies are based on psychological, communication, and human behavior concepts. Let us look at some of the most successful ones and how to use them:

1. Mutuality

The reciprocity principle is founded on the premise that individuals feel compelled to give back to those who have given to them initially. This principle is very important in negotiations. When you make a goodwill gesture or provide concessions, your opponent is more inclined to reciprocate.

In a pay discussion, for example, if you're ready to be flexible on some perks, your counterpart may be more likely to reciprocate by giving a higher base income. The important thing is to make the first approach and show a willingness to compromise.

2. Dearth

Scarcity is a strong psychological motivator. When individuals believe that something is in short supply, they place a higher value on it and move rapidly to obtain it. This approach may be used to generate a feeling of urgency in negotiations.

Scarcity may be used in business negotiations by suggesting that a certain offer or discount is only accessible for a limited period. This may persuade your rival to act sooner rather than later.

3. Possession of authority

People are more likely to heed the advice of reliable, competent specialists. This concept is about establishing oneself as an expert in your industry or using reputable sources to back up your claims.

When negotiating a contract, you might use industry standards, legislation, or famous experts in your sector to back up your offers. This lends credibility to your stance and may influence the choice of your rival.

4. Consistency and dedication

Humans have a great need to be consistent in their acts and statements. When a person makes a commitment or takes a stance, they are more likely to follow through on it. This idea may be used to your advantage in negotiations.

Start by persuading your adversary to agree on minor topics or commitments connected to the discussion. They are more likely to be consistent and agree to greater demands that match their earlier commitments after they have committed to these.

5. Social Evidence

People often seek to others for advice on how to act. When individuals witness others adopting a certain activity, they are more likely to follow suit. Social evidence may be a powerful negotiating tool.

Application: During a commercial discussion, you may present instances of comparable agreements that have benefitted other organizations or people. This indicates that your plan is a popular and successful option, which makes it more appealing to your competitor.

6. Appreciation

Those they like may convince them more readily. Developing rapport and a favorable connection with your adversary may make or break the negotiating process.

Spend some time getting to know your adversary on a personal level. Discover shared hobbies or relationships that may foster liking and trust. This personal connection may impact their desire to collaborate with you.

7. Anchoring and framing

How you phrase information and the first anchor you establish may have a significant influence on a negotiation. Framing is the process of presenting information in such a manner that it impacts how it is viewed, while anchoring is the act of providing the initial offer or figure, which serves as a reference point.

When negotiating a product's price, try presenting it as a cost per usage, emphasizing the long-term benefit. Set a high anchor price first, which will make future offers seem more acceptable to your competitor.

Storytelling is the eighth skill.

Storytelling is an emotional method that makes your message more relevant. Humans are inherently attracted to tales, and they may be an effective approach to communicating your message.

Use narrative to demonstrate the possible advantages of your proposition during negotiations. Share real-life examples, case studies, or personal tales that show how your plan has made a difference.

Active Listening is the ninth skill.

Active listening is a persuasive strategy as well as a critical component of good communication. When you listen carefully to your opponent, you show that you appreciate their viewpoint and are eager to participate in a healthy debate.

Application: Make a concerted effort to actively listen to what your adversary is saying during a negotiation. Empathetic comments demonstrate that you understand their worries and are willing to establish common ground.

10. Recognition and Validation

Acknowledgment and validation are effective persuasive strategies that respect your counterpart's feelings and points of view. People are more open to your ideas when they feel heard and valued.

Recognize your counterpart's sentiments and point of view if they raise worries or objections. Respond by supporting their point of view, which helps reduce tension and open them up to your recommended solutions.

Using Multiple Persuasive Techniques

While each of these persuasive strategies is useful on its own, their actual effectiveness frequently comes from carefully combining them. The strategies you employ and how you mix them should be influenced by your knowledge of your opponent, their goals, and the negotiating dynamics.

In a commercial transaction, for example, you may begin by establishing your authority via industry expertise and references. You may then leverage reciprocity by granting a concession, such as extending payment terms, to persuade your counterpart to reciprocate. Active listening and recognition throughout the discussion legitimize your counterpart's concerns and create trust.

Finally, the art of persuasion is an important talent in bargaining. It is built on the principles of human psychology and successful communication. Persuasive approaches, when applied ethically and intelligently, may help you create win-win results, establish solid connections, and design solutions that serve the interests of all parties involved. Finally, persuasion is about encouraging people to accept your point of view rather than pushing them to do so.

Chapter 5: Handling Conflict and Difficult Situations

Negotiations often involve challenging moments and conflicts. In this chapter, we'll discuss strategies for managing difficult situations, dealing with aggressive or passive counterparts, and overcoming obstacles that may arise during negotiations. By the end of this chapter, you'll be better equipped to navigate the rough waters of negotiation with grace and confidence.

As we've seen, negotiation is a complex ballet of strategy, persuasion, and human dynamics. However, like with any dance, there will be blunders and periods of disharmony. In this chapter, we will explore conflict and challenging circumstances that often happen during negotiations. We'll talk about how to cope with these issues, how to deal with aggressive or passive rivals, and how to overcome roadblocks that may endanger the smooth course of negotiations. You'll be able to sail the turbulent seas of negotiation with elegance and confidence by the conclusion of this chapter.

Conflict Is a Natural Part of Negotiation

Conflict is an unavoidable component of the negotiating process. It occurs when the interests of the persons involved collide, and it may take many forms, ranging from differences of opinion and expectations to open confrontations. However, it is important to recognize that conflict does not have to be negative; it may catalyze constructive problem-solving and progress.

What Causes Conflict:

Differing Interests: Each side in a negotiation brings its own set of interests and aims to the table. Conflict may emerge when these interests do not coincide.

Miscommunication: Conflict may arise as a result of poor communication or misconceptions. Messages may be misconstrued, or critical information may be overlooked.

Emotional Factors: Emotions are important in conflict. Frustration, wrath, or fear may exacerbate arguments and make logical decision-making difficult.

Lack of Trust: When there is a lack of trust, parties are more likely to regard each other's behavior with mistrust, escalating small conflicts into significant ones.

While disagreement is unavoidable, how it is handled may be the difference between a successful and unsuccessful negotiation. Conflict resolution skills may lead to innovative solutions and the development of relationships.

Conflict Resolution Techniques

Active listening is one of the most successful methods of dispute resolution. Giving your undivided attention to your adversary shows that you value their viewpoint. This may help to de-escalate tensions and foster understanding.

When a quarrel arises, attentively listen to your counterpart's concerns. Repeat what you've heard to ensure you grasp their perspective. This demonstrates that you appreciate their perspective and are open to engaging in meaningful debate.

Empathetic Reactions: Empathy is a great conflict resolution strategy. It entails understanding and respecting your counterpart's feelings. People's emotional reactions tend to soften when they feel heard and understood.

Respond with empathy if your opponent displays irritation or anxiety. Recognize their emotions and validate their point of view. By way of example, you may say, "I understand that this **situation is frustrating for you, and I want to work together to find a solution."**

Approach to Problem Solving: Conflict often revolves around particular topics or disparities in interests. You may change the attention from disagreement to finding mutually beneficial solutions by using a problem-solving technique.

Application: Encourage your partner to discover the root causes of the disagreement. Then, collaborate to generate alternative solutions that solve these challenges while also being in the best interests of both sides.

Maintain Your Cool: Emotional reactions may aggravate conflict. It is critical to be cool and controlled while dealing with disagreement. This may aid in de-escalation and foster sensible discourse.

When confronted with a quarrel, take a minute to gather your thoughts and manage your emotions. Respond with a controlled and calm approach, which may help to create a favorable tone for the debate.

Establish Ground Rules: Setting ground rules for communication may be especially beneficial in high-conflict settings. These guidelines may include taking turns speaking, refraining from personal insults, and concentrating on the problems at hand.

Application: If the negotiation is becoming heated, consider establishing ground rules for the conversation. You may, for example, suggest that each side take turns voicing their concerns without interruption.

Seek Mediation: In circumstances when disagreement is chronic or complicated, involving a neutral third party to mediate the debate may be advantageous. A mediator may assist in facilitating communication and guiding the negotiation to a successful conclusion.

If the disagreement is still unsolved, try offering mediation to your opponent. A professional mediator may assist both parties in exploring alternatives and reaching an agreement.

Dealing with Aggressive Opponents

In negotiations, aggressive competitors may provide a unique difficulty. Their boldness and combative manner may create a hostile environment and make finding common ground difficult. Dealing with such people requires a calculated and deliberate strategy.

Techniques for Dealing with Aggressive Opponents:

Stay Calm and Assertive: When confronted with hostility, it's critical to keep your cool. Respond assertively rather than aggressively. Firm yet courteous assertive speech might help diffuse anger.

If your opponent gets confrontational, answer with, "I understand your concerns, and I'm here to collaborate on a solution." Let us concentrate on the problems at hand."

Establish Limits: Establish clear communication limits. Inform the aggressive party, politely but firmly, that certain actions, such as personal assaults or yelling, are inappropriate.

In the face of aggressiveness, you may say, "I'm open to discussing our differences, but I'm not going to engage in personal attacks or shouting." Let us keep our conversation civil."

Pay attention to Understand: Investigate the underlying motives behind the aggressive conduct. Is it motivated by dissatisfaction, fear, or a desire for a competitive advantage? Listening to their concerns might assist you in addressing the underlying reasons for their hostility.

If your competitor acts aggressively, attentively listen to their issues and offer clarifying questions. "I see you're passionate about this issue," for example. Can you explain why it's so essential to you?"

Discover Common Ground: Look for points of agreement or common interests. By stressing common ground, you may steer the conversation away from conflict and toward cooperation.

When confronted with violence, shift the discourse toward common aims or interests. For example, "While we may disagree, we both want this project to succeed." Let us concentrate on how we can collaborate to make it happen."

Try taking Breaks When Necessary: If the aggressiveness gets unbearable and effective discussion becomes impossible, try taking a break. A quick break might give both sides a chance to cool down and recover.

Application: If the conversation turns heated, propose a little pause to your colleague. This pause may enable emotions to calm and allow for more productive communication when the conversation resumes.

Involve a Third Party: In cases when violence continues and settlement seems improbable, using a mediator or impartial third party may be advantageous. Their presence may serve to reduce tension and steer the discussion in a more positive direction.

Application: If a negotiation with an aggressive rival hits a stalemate, consider bringing in a mediator or third party to help facilitate the conversation.

Managing Passive Counterparts

While assertiveness might be tough, passivity poses its own set of challenges in negotiations. Passive opponents may avoid confrontation, be hesitant to communicate their desires or be indecisive, making agreement difficult. A particular set of methods is required to successfully negotiate with passive folks.

Approaches to Dealing with Passive Counterparts:

Encourage Open Communication: Make the setting secure and friendly for passive counterparts to express themselves. Assure them that their ideas and concerns are taken into consideration.

To promote open discussion, say something like, "I appreciate your input, and I'd like to hear your thoughts on this." Please feel free to share your thoughts."

Pose Wide-Open Questions: Passive people may feel more at ease answering open-ended questions that enable them to express themselves freely. These questions allow people to express their emotions and opinions.

Open-ended queries may be used to extract information and views from passive counterparts. Like the question, "How do you envision this project progressing, and what are your main concerns?"

Provide Options: Offering options may empower passive competitors and engage them in the negotiation. You offer them a feeling of control by giving alternatives.

Provide various options to passive counterparts while debating a decision. This may be as easy as stating, "Here are some options for us to consider." Which one do you think best matches your preferences?"

Establish Clear Expectations: Outline the expectations for the negotiating process in detail. This offers structure to passive persons and a better knowledge of their position in the negotiation.

Establish clear expectations by expressing, "Our goal in this negotiation is to reach an agreement that benefits both parties." Your feedback is critical to reaching this aim, so please don't be shy about sharing your ideas."

Be patient: Understand that passive peers may take longer to make choices or communicate their opinions. Avoid hurrying them, since this might create pain and reluctance.

Allow passive counterparts enough time to analyze information and make judgments. Show patience by stating, "Take your time considering our options, and let me know when you're ready to discuss further."

Highlight the Advantages: Emphasize the advantages of the proposed agreement or plan of action. Passive people may be more likely to participate if they perceive favorable effects.

When proposing a plan, emphasize the pros and benefits. It is possible to say, "By agreeing to this, we can achieve these positive outcomes that align with our shared goals."

Overcoming Difficulties

During negotiations, obstacles might take many shapes. External forces, unanticipated hurdles, or arguments may all stymie development. Overcoming these challenges requires flexibility, problem-solving abilities, and good communication.

Overcoming Obstacles Strategies:

Identify and Understand the difficulty: Identifying and understanding the difficulty is the first step in conquering it. What is producing the stumbling block? Is it a misunderstanding, a lack of knowledge, or something else?

Take the time to consider the nature of the barrier. Discuss it with your counterpart to get a common understanding of the problem.

Collaborative Problem-Solving: Collaborate with your counterpart to solve problems. Collaborate on potential ideas and look for common ground to solve the problem.

Start a problem-solving conversation with your counterpart. Encourage them to share their ideas on how to overcome the problem and collaborate to find a solution.

Communication and Flexibility: When challenges develop, effective communication is critical. Maintain open channels of communication and be adaptable in your approach to problem-solving.

Maintain open and straightforward communication with your opponent. As you attempt to overcome the impediment, be open to alter your plan and adapt to new conditions.

Leverage other Resources: To overcome hurdles, you may need to use other resources or skills. This might include consulting with experts, consultants, or mentors.

Application: If the problem necessitates specific expertise or resources, consider contacting outside specialists who may provide advice and solutions.

Reassess and adjust: When a barrier persists, you must reconsider your strategy. Are there any other options or concessions that might help you go forward?

Reassess your bargaining approach and explore changes that may assist you in overcoming the roadblock. Be willing to consider compromise and other solutions.

Maintain a Positive Attitude: A positive attitude may be a great motivator when it comes to conquering problems. Maintain a positive attitude and faith in your capacity to solve problems.

Approach challenges with a good attitude and confidence. Remember that overcoming obstacles is a normal part of the bargaining process.

Conclusion

Conflict and unpleasant circumstances are unavoidable in the realm of negotiation. They do not, however, have to be insurmountable. You may successfully handle these problems with the correct methods and a good grasp of human dynamics.

Handling disagreement with elegance and firmness is a talent that may lead to mutually beneficial agreements and enhance relationships, whether with aggressive or passive rivals. Overcoming hurdles in negotiations requires adaptation, problem-solving, and clear communication.

By understanding these methods, you will be better prepared to handle the complexities of negotiation, transforming possible roadblocks into stepping stones on your way to success. Remember that negotiating is about more than simply getting the best deal; it's about developing and sustaining meaningful connections that may lead to career and financial success.

Chapter 6: Negotiating for Career Advancement

Few abilities are as important as bargaining on the road of life and career. Whether you're a fresh graduate starting your career or a seasoned worker trying to advance, your skill to bargain may have a significant influence on your career growth. This chapter focuses on how negotiating may be a powerful tool for boosting your professional career. We'll go into the intricacies of pay negotiations, obtaining promotions, and positioning yourself for success within your firm. By the conclusion of this chapter, you'll have a thorough grasp of how to use negotiation to advance your career.

Negotiation's Role in Career Advancement

Before we get into the intricacies of job-related negotiations, it's important to understand the function of negotiation in professional progression. Negotiation in a professional environment is fundamentally about arguing for yourself and your interests inside the professional arena. It's a way to get not just the work you want, but also the pay, perks, and prospects that line with your objectives and values.

Why Negotiation Is Important for Career Advancement:

Maximizing Compensation: By negotiating your pay and benefits, you may guarantee that you are being properly and equitably paid for your abilities and accomplishments.

Securing Advancements: When competing for promotions, increases, or leadership positions, negotiation is vital. It allows you to exhibit your worth and dedication to the company.

Profession Development: By negotiating, you may find chances for training, skill development, and mentoring that can help you advance in your profession.

Building Confidence: Negotiation improves your self-confidence, allowing you to show yourself as a skilled professional.

Negotiation helps you to match your professional trajectory with your long-term objectives, ensuring your career is on the proper track.

Salary Discussions

Salary discussions are an important part of advancing in your job. A well-negotiated pay not only affects your present financial situation but also sets the scene for future earnings and professional advancement.

Salary Negotiation Preparation:

Research industry norms and compensation benchmarks for your job before initiating wage negotiations. Websites such as Glassdoor and Payscale may give useful information.

Know Your Worth: Be honest about your abilities, expertise, and credentials. Understand your organization's unique worth and how it converts into market value.

Set specific goals: Establish your desired pay and perks. Prepare to explain why you feel you are entitled to receive compensation.

Consider the Bigger Picture: Take into account the whole remuneration package, including perks, bonuses, stock options, and opportunities for advancement. It is not only about the starting wage.

During Salary Discussions:

Value Emphasis: Highlight the value you contribute to the company. Highlight your achievements and talents, as well as how they contribute to the development of the organization.

Exhibit Confidence: Go into the negotiation with confidence. This does not imply arrogance, but rather confidence in your value and ability to negotiate a reasonable salary package.

Active listening: Take note of your employer's comments and counter-offers. Prepare to participate in a productive conversation.

Negotiate the Total Package: Don't only focus on the compensation. Benefits like as health insurance, retirement contributions, flexible work arrangements, and performance-based incentives should be negotiated.

Prepare to Walk Away: While you desire the job, you must be prepared to walk away if the offer does not meet your expectations. This position might reflect your dedication to obtaining a fair bargain.

Seek Win-Win Results: Negotiations are not a conflict; they are a collaborative effort. Seek win-win ideas that benefit both you and your company.

Following Salary Negotiations:

Ensure that the agreed-upon conditions are memorialized in writing, often in an offer letter. This helps to prevent future misunderstandings.

Regardless of the result, express thanks for the chance to join the company and the negotiating process.

Maintain an Open Line of Communication: Maintain open and good contact with your employer, and keep proving your worth via your job.

Promotional Negotiation

A promotion is often the next stage in your professional growth. Promotions represent not just more responsibility and power but also increased recognition and income. Here's how to handle promotion negotiations:

Promotion Negotiation Preparation:

Assess Your Readiness: Determine if you are actually prepared for the promotion. Consider your abilities, expertise, and contributions to the company.

Understand the criteria: Familiarize yourself with the new role's expectations and criteria. Prepare to describe how you will meet or surpass them.

Quantify Achievements: Provide actual proof of your present role's successes. To illustrate your influence, provide facts and concrete examples.

Build connections: Develop good connections with organizational decision-makers. A solid network may lead to possibilities for advancement.

During Promotional Talks:

Express Your Interest: Inform your superiors that you are interested in the promotion. Be upfront and explicit about your goals.

Make a compelling case: Make a persuasive argument for your promotion, emphasizing how your talents and expertise match the needs of the new position.

Showcase Your Positive Influence: Highlight the positive influence you've made in your present job. Explain how your donations have helped the organization.

Demonstrate Enthusiasm: Express your eagerness to take on additional duties and contribute to the success of the business.

Negotiate remuneration: Talk about the remuneration package that comes with the promotion. This might be a pay raise, a bonus, or stock options.

Request Feedback: Seek comments on your performance and any areas where you may improve. It might be advantageous to demonstrate a dedication to progress.

Following Promotional Negotiations:

Seek Clarity: Ensure that you have a thorough knowledge of the promotion's conditions and expectations.

Deliver outcomes: Once you've landed the promotion, concentrate on proving your value by providing excellent outcomes in your new job.

Maintain Professionalism: As you move into your new role, maintain professionalism and a pleasant attitude.

Continue Developing: Even after you have been promoted, you should continue to grow your abilities and extend your knowledge in order to flourish in your new job.

Positioning Your Organization for Success

Career growth is about placing yourself for long-term success inside your firm, not only winning promotions or pay increases. Here are some techniques to assist you chart a course that will lead you to your objectives:

1. Establish Specific Goals: Define your professional objectives and desires. This clarity will drive your organizational choices and activities.

2. Seek input: Seek input from your supervisors, peers, and subordinates on a regular basis. Constructive criticism may give useful insights for future improvements.

3. Lifelong Learning: Make a commitment to lifelong learning and skill improvement. Keep up to date on industry trends and upcoming technology.

4. Networking: Develop a strong professional network both inside and outside of your business. Mentorship and opportunity may be obtained via networking.

5. Take the initiative: Propose new ideas, changes, or initiatives that will benefit the company. Proactivity is often rewarded.

6. Problem-Solving: Solve problems. Provide answers to problems in your department or company. Your capacity to solve problems may set you apart as a valued asset.

7. Adaptability: Be adaptive and open to new experiences. The corporate world is always changing, and those that accept change do well.

8. Leadership abilities: Even if you are not in a formal leadership position, you should develop leadership abilities. Organizations place a high emphasis on effective leadership abilities.

9. Professionalism: Maintain a professional demeanor in your relationships and job. Trust is built via consistency in your conduct and job excellence.

10. Recognize and exploit Your talents: Recognize and exploit your talents in your position. Align your obligations with your strengths.

11. Give recognition: Recognize and recognize coworkers and team members for their efforts. This encourages a good, collaborative work atmosphere.

12. Seek Mentorship: Seek advice from seasoned individuals inside your business. A mentor may provide advice and insights to help you advance in your profession.

13. Time Management: Balance your work and personal lives by effectively managing your time. Long-term success might be hampered by burnout.

14. Create a Personal Brand: Create a personal brand that corresponds with your job objectives. It is important to consider your reputation and how you are seen inside the company.

Conclusion

Negotiating for job progress is a complicated path that includes pay discussions, promotion opportunities, and positioning oneself for long-term success. Your profession is an important aspect of your life, and your ability to negotiate within it may be a spark for reaching your goals and financial success. Remember that negotiating is about more than simply obtaining favorable terms; it is also about arguing for your interests and establishing your worth in your professional path. Mastering the art of negotiating in your work opens the door to a future full of opportunity and personal satisfaction.

Chapter 7: Negotiating for Financial Success

Welcome to the last part of our trip, in which we will look at how negotiating can be a strong instrument that has a direct influence on your financial well-being. Negotiation, as you've seen throughout this course, is a flexible ability that can be used in a variety of situations. It's no different when it comes to your money. Negotiation techniques apply whether you're purchasing a house, investing in stocks, or establishing a company. In this chapter, we'll look at financial discussions, such as purchasing and selling assets, investing techniques, and structuring win-win financial transactions. You will be better positioned to ensure your financial future and attain the degree of financial success you seek if you grasp these fundamentals.

Negotiation's Importance in Financial Success

Negotiation is important in the area of finance and asset management. It's all about obtaining the greatest discounts, making wise financial choices, and eventually improving your financial situation. Here are some of the reasons why negotiating is essential for financial success:

Maximizing Value: When purchasing or selling assets, getting loans, or making investments, negotiation may help you maximize the value of your financial transactions.

Risk Mitigation: Effective negotiating may help you minimize financial risks by ensuring that you make educated and measured decisions.

Wealth Creation: You may generate prospects for wealth accumulation and financial development by negotiating advantageous terms and circumstances.

Asset Management: Negotiation is an essential component of asset management, ensuring that your assets are performing properly to create profits and protect your financial future.

Strategic Planning: Through negotiation, you may successfully strategize and plan your financial actions, aligning them with your long-term financial objectives.

Purchasing and Selling Assets

Whether it's a home, a vehicle, or a work of art, purchasing and selling assets often involves large financial transactions. The skill to properly bargain may result in significant savings when acquiring or improved earnings when selling. Here's how to handle asset purchase and sale negotiations:

Purchasing Assets:

Complete Your Homework: Investigate the market and the exact asset you wish to purchase. Understand its current market worth and circumstances.

Set a Budget: Establish your budget and the most you're willing to spend on the asset. Prepare to stay with it.

Propose: Present your offer to the seller, preferably after properly evaluating the item. Your offer should be reasonable yet provide space for bargaining.

Value should be highlighted: When making your offer, underline the value you provide as a buyer. Explain why the asset is a suitable match for you and any unique benefits you can provide.

Be patient: Negotiation may include counteroffers and back-and-forth conversations. Be patient and open to productive discussion.

Use Leverage: Determine any circumstances that provide you with bargaining power. It might be your swift decision-making abilities, readiness to pay in cash, or the unique terms you can give.

Seek Win-Win Solutions: Approach the negotiation as a collaborative effort to achieve a win-win solution. This might increase goodwill and assist the transaction.

Don't Be Hasty: Avoid making a hasty purchase. Take your time evaluating the item and negotiating carefully.

Assets for Sale:

Know Your Asset: Understand the asset's market worth as well as any distinctive qualities or benefits it provides. This information will assist you in determining an acceptable selling price.

Prepare for Negotiation: Expect prospective purchasers to bargain. Prepare to deal with counteroffers and discussions in a professional manner.

Set a Competitive Price: To maximize your profit, you must first establish a competitive and realistic selling price. Buyers may be put off by an exorbitant price.

Emphasize Value: When offering your item for sale, emphasize its worth and what distinguishes it from others on the market.

Market Effectively: Invest in marketing and presentation to increase the attraction of your item. Buyers might be enticed by high-quality photographs and detailed descriptions.

Negotiate Professionally: When negotiating, be professional and courteous. Maintain open conversation and propose mutually beneficial compromises.

Assess Buyer Motivation: Learn about the buyer's motivations and reasons for buying. This knowledge may help you plan your bargaining approach.

Seek Professional Help: To guarantee a successful sale of complicated or high-value assets, seek help from financial advisers or real estate specialists.

Investment Techniques

Investing is a critical component of financial success. Whether you invest in stocks, real estate, or other assets, your ability to bargain successfully may have a substantial influence on your investment results. Here are some tactics for bargaining in the financial world:

Stock Market Bargaining:

Diversify Your Portfolio: A key tactic in stock market negotiating is diversification. To limit risk, diversify your assets across industries and asset types.

Set specific investment objectives: Determine your investing objectives and time frame. Do you want short-term profits or long-term growth? Your financial selections should be guided by your objectives.

Stay Informed: Stay up to date on the businesses and sectors in which you are investing. Learn about their financial health, competitive position, and future development opportunities.

Buy cheap, Sell High: This traditional investing approach includes acquiring assets at cheap prices and selling them at high ones. In stock market negotiations, timing is everything.

Use Stop-Loss Orders: Use stop-loss orders to protect your assets by automatically selling a stock if its price falls below a specific threshold. This helps to reduce any losses.

Establish Realistic Expectations: Recognize that the stock market may be turbulent. Set reasonable return expectations and be prepared for market swings.

Negotiating a Real Estate Investment:

Choose the Best Location: When it comes to real estate investing, location is everything. Investigate and choose properties in locations with high development and demand.

Understand the Market: Be knowledgeable about the real estate market in your desired area. Understand property prices, possible rental revenue, and market trends.

Inspect Properties: Carefully examine the properties in which you wish to invest. Determine any necessary repairs or improvements and include them in your negotiations.

Purchase Price Negotiation: When acquiring real estate, negotiate the purchase price and conditions. If the original offer isn't favorable, be ready to make a counteroffer.

Rent Negotiations: If you are investing in rental properties, professionally negotiate rental prices with renters. Make your lease conditions and expectations clear.

Negotiate property management rates and services with management firms if you are not managing the property yourself.

Seek Legal and Financial Advice: Real estate investments might be difficult to understand. Seek legal and financial guidance to ensure your investments are properly organized.

Negotiating a Business Investment:

Due Diligence: When investing in a company, do extensive due diligence. Examine its financials, prospects for development, and industry position.

Negotiate conditions: Whether it's stock ownership, loan conditions, or another kind of investment, negotiate the terms of your investment. Check if the terms are clear and beneficial.

Partnership Agreements: If you're forming a partnership, you should draft partnership agreements outlining duties, obligations, and profit allocation.

Departure plans: Think about and negotiate your departure plans. What if you decide to sell your company investment? Plan your departure strategies ahead of time.

Identify and manage the risks involved with your company investment. Create risk-mitigation methods and include them in your investment agreement.

Professional Assistance: To handle the complexity of large company investments, seek the help of financial specialists, attorneys, and business consultants.

Creating Win-Win Financial Transactions

Negotiating aims to create win-win scenarios in which all parties gain. This idea is still important in financial talks. Here are some ways to negotiate win-win financial transactions:

Identify common aims: Identify common aims or interests in any financial transaction. Knowing what each party wants may lead to mutually beneficial solutions.

Maintain open and honest communication throughout the negotiating process. Encourage the other person to communicate their wants and concerns.

Build Trust: Successful financial talks are built on trust. Build trust by being honest, having integrity, and following through on your commitments.

Seek Creative ideas: Be open to innovative ideas that benefit both parties. Flexibility may lead to novel and mutually beneficial transactions.

Negotiate many topics: Many financial discussions include many topics. Consider the whole package, including the price, conditions, and extra perks.

Consider the Long-Term Consequences: Consider the deal's long-term repercussions. Will it lead to a long-term and pleasant relationship for both parties?

Professional Mediation: In complicated discussions, consider hiring a professional mediator or negotiator to assist both sides in establishing common ground.

Fairness is important: Strive for fairness in the negotiation. A fair agreement benefits both parties and sets the tone for future encounters.

Conclusion

In this last chapter, we looked at how negotiating may help you achieve financial success. Negotiation techniques apply whether you're buying and selling goods, investing, or making win-win financial arrangements. Your financial well-being is determined not just by the amount of money you earn, but also by the financial choices you make and the effectiveness with which you negotiate them.

Remember that financial bargaining is about more than simply generating money; it's about ensuring your financial future and opening up prospects for wealth building. You'll be better equipped to manage the complicated world of finance and accomplish your financial objectives if you follow the tactics and ideas presented in this chapter. Finally, bargaining is the key to succeeding in the ever-changing field of personal money and asset management.

*

www.ingramcontent.com/pod-product-compliance
Lightning Source LLC
Chambersburg PA
CBHW062240290526
45794CB00006B/2354